by Barbara Klimowicz

WHEN

SHOES EAT SOCKS

Pictures BY GLORIA KAMEN

ABINGDON PRESS   Nashville · New York

WHEN SHOES EAT SOCKS

For my nieces and nephews

There was something terribly wrong with little Barnaby's shoes. They ate his socks. Yes, they did! They ate his socks.

The first time he noticed it was when Big Roy and Baggie Maggie and Scooter asked him to play Follow-the-Cat. It seemed to little Barnaby that he had been waiting forever for Big Roy and Baggie Maggie and Scooter to ask him. They thought he was too little to play, but he just knew he could do what they did. Big Roy was the Cat. Everyone had to follow the Cat.

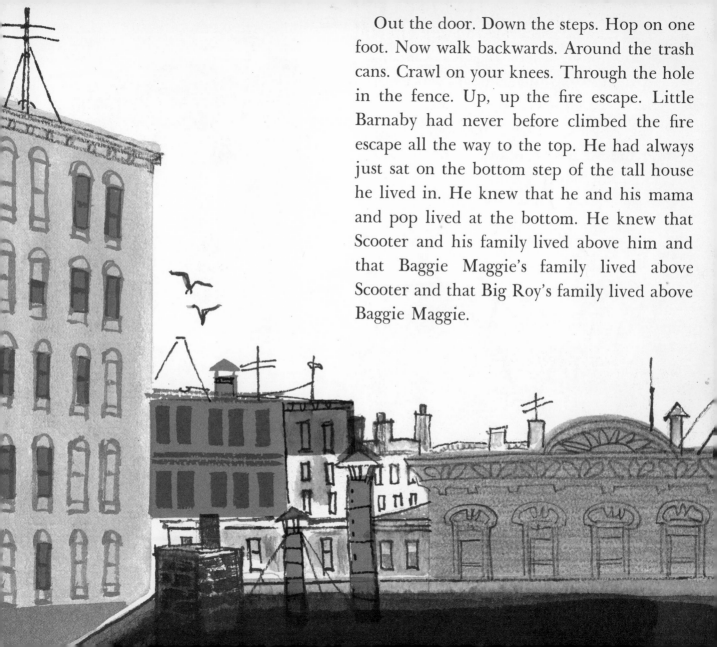

Out the door. Down the steps. Hop on one foot. Now walk backwards. Around the trash cans. Crawl on your knees. Through the hole in the fence. Up, up the fire escape. Little Barnaby had never before climbed the fire escape all the way to the top. He had always just sat on the bottom step of the tall house he lived in. He knew that he and his mama and pop lived at the bottom. He knew that Scooter and his family lived above him and that Baggie Maggie's family lived above Scooter and that Big Roy's family lived above Baggie Maggie.

Now here he was up at the very top of the tall house, where Big Roy's mama gave them each a gingersnap to eat. Little Barnaby would have liked to stay up high in Big Roy's apartment and look out of the windows for birds and jet planes and clouds. But Big Roy said, "Heck, all you can see are other people's windows." Big Roy was the Cat, and the Cat was in a hurry.

Down a flight of steps. Through Baggie
Maggie's mother's kitchen. Eat a big jelly
doughnut. Down another flight. Through
Scooter's mother's kitchen. Eat a cold pan-
cake. Down another flight. Through little
Barnaby's mother's kitchen. Eat a prune.
Sit on the bottom step. Spit the prune pit
a million miles. Get up. Turn a somer-
sault. And that's when it happened!

"Wait for me!" said little Barnaby.

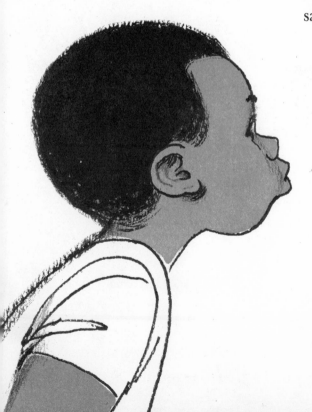

"Hurry up, little Barnaby."
"You got to keep up if you want t[
play."
"Yeah, little Barnaby."
"But something awful happened!

Big Roy and Baggie Maggie and Scooter came back to the bottom step.

"What happened?"

"You sick?"

"You lose something?"

Little Barnaby was staring at his feet. "L-l-look," he stammered in awe. "My shoes ate my socks!"

Everyone stared at little Barnaby's shoes.

"Well, I declare!" said Big Roy.

"Those are sure some hungry shoes!" said Baggie Maggie.

"They're just like hungry puppy dogs," said Scooter. "Puppy dogs like to chew socks."

Little Barnaby slapped playfully at his shoes. "Hey, you puppy dogs!" he said. "Quit eating my socks! Hear?"

Then he had to take off his shoes and pull his socks back up over his heels and put his shoes back on.

That was the first time. But after that his shoes got hungrier and hungrier. They were always eating his socks.

One day Big Roy and Baggie Maggie and Scooter and little Barnaby were playing Kick-the-Can. First Big Roy kicked it. Then Baggie Maggie kicked it. Then Scooter kicked it. Then little Barnaby kicked it. Then kick and kick and kick and . . .

"Hey, little Barnaby!"
"What for you sitting down?"
"Your turn, little Barnaby!"
Little Barnaby looked scared. He
pointed to his feet. Sure enough. His
shoes were eating his socks again.

"I'm tired of your shoes!" said Big Roy.

"If you'd just tie them, your socks wouldn't scootch down like that," said Baggie Maggie, stooping down to help little Barnaby.

"I don't know how to tie shoes."

"Well, you ought to learn," said Baggie Maggie.

"I think your shoes are wild animals," said Scooter. "Grrr! They open up their big mouths and then gobble-gobble-go-your-socks. Pretty soon they'll eat your toes."

Little Barnaby's eyes grew big.

"Aw, don't pay attention," said Baggie Maggie. "He's just teasing."

But little Barnaby couldn't forget what Scooter had said. Every night when he went to sleep, he thought about his shoes under his bed. They were wild animals waiting in the dark for morning to come so they could eat his socks again, and maybe his toes.

Every morning little Barnaby's mama said, "When you going to learn to tie your own shoes, little boy?" But Barnaby was always in a hurry to run outdoors to play, and he wouldn't wait for his mama to teach him.

"When you going to learn to tie those shoes?" his pop would say when he saw little Barnaby's shoestrings trailing on the floor. But little Barnaby was always in a hurry to run outdoors to play, and he wouldn't wait for his pop to teach him.

Baggie Maggie tried time and time again to get little Barnaby to sit down on the bottom step and learn to tie his shoes.

"Now watch," she'd say. "Make a rabbit's ear with this string, then wrap it round with this other string and hunt for the other rabbit's ear and pull it through. There, doesn't that look pretty?"

But little Barnaby's eyes weren't watching the rabbit's ears. They were busy watching Big Roy do cartwheels or Scooter roll an old tire around.

One day Big Roy and Baggie Maggie and Scooter and little Barnaby played Marching Band. Big Roy came first twirling a mop handle. Then came Baggie Maggie playing tissue paper on a comb. Then came Scooter tooting on a funnel. Last came little Barnaby banging a spoon on a pan. Past the pawn shop, past the shoeshine, past the newsstand, past the delicatessen they marched. Past the empty store and the other empty store and the fruit stand and Tiny's Spaghetti Place.

Then the spoon stopped banging on the pan, and the rest of the Marching Band stopped and turned around. There was little Barnaby sitting in the middle of the sidewalk. He was so scared he could hardly talk.

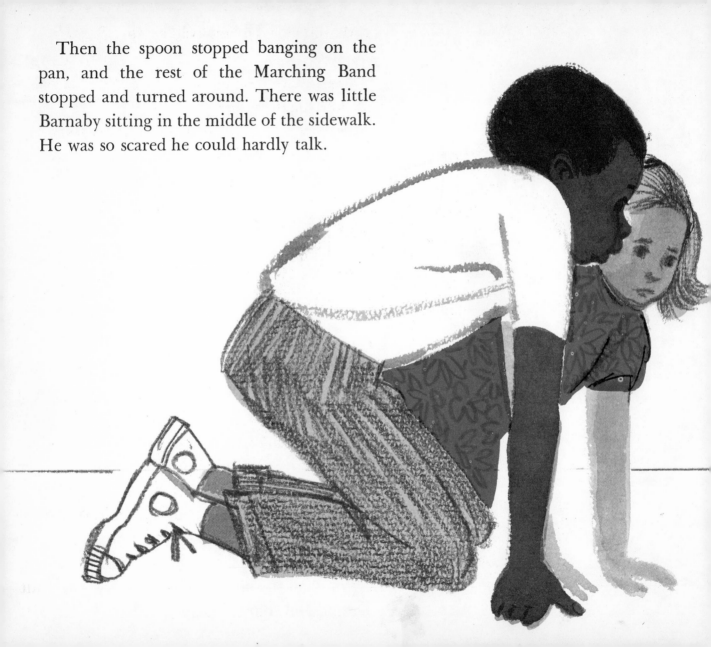

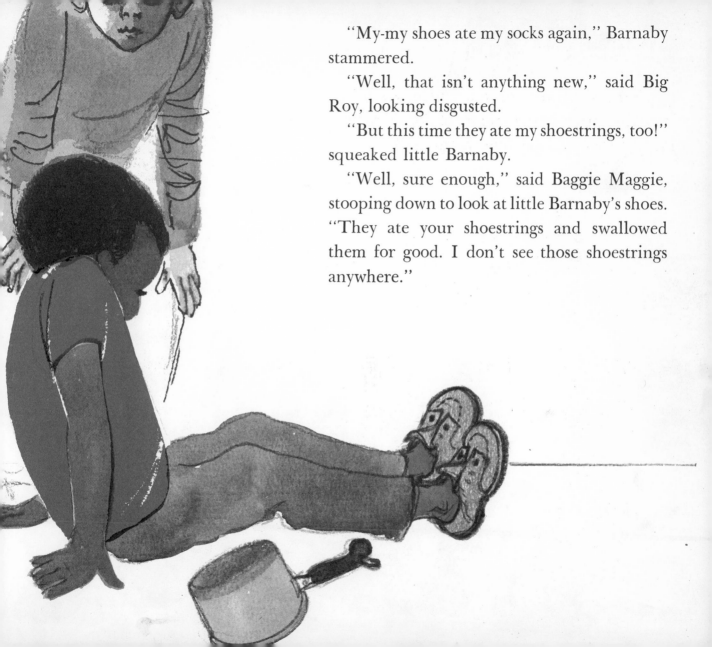

"My-my shoes ate my socks again," Barnaby stammered.

"Well, that isn't anything new," said Big Roy, looking disgusted.

"But this time they ate my shoestrings, too!" squeaked little Barnaby.

"Well, sure enough," said Baggie Maggie, stooping down to look at little Barnaby's shoes. "They ate your shoestrings and swallowed them for good. I don't see those shoestrings anywhere."

"Your shoes are monsters!" said Scooter.
"Look at their big flappy tongues sticking out.
You'd better not wear those monster shoes
anymore. They might swallow your toes and
your heels and your ankles and your knees
and . . ."

"Cut it out," said Baggie Maggie to Scooter.
"You're scaring Barnaby. He's just teasing,
little Barnaby."

"Well, anyhow," said Big Roy. "We're not playing with you anymore. Pull up your socks and go on home. When you learn to tie your shoes, then you'll be big enough to play with us again."

With that the marching band marched down the sidewalk and around the corner out of sight. Little Barnaby was left alone. He took off his monster shoes with shaking fingers and pulled up his socks. But he was afraid to put the monsters back on his feet. So he put them in his pan with the spoon and walked home in his sock feet.

When he got home, he put the monsters in the pan in his bedroom closet and shut the door tight. He banged on the closet door with his spoon and said in a fierce voice, "You stay in there and don't you ever come out. You hear?"

But now little Barnaby didn't have any shoes to wear or any friends to play with. So he went to bed.

His mama thought he was sick. She put her hand on his head to see if it was hot. She brought him chicken broth on a tray for supper.

Little Barnaby's pop came and kissed him goodnight and turned out the light. But little Barnaby couldn't sleep. He knew the monsters were in the closet. Scooter said they might swallow his toes and his heels and his ankles and his knees with their long flappy tongues.

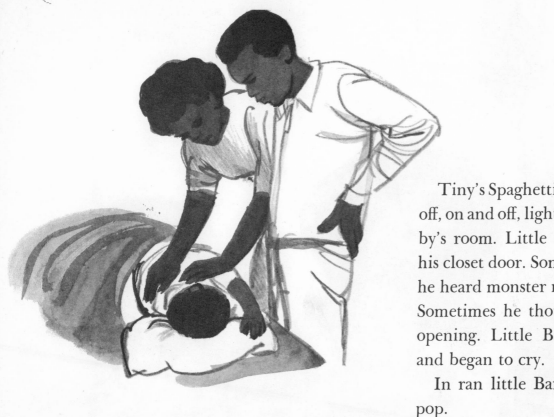

Tiny's Spaghetti sign flashed on and off, on and off, lighting up little Barnaby's room. Little Barnaby could see his closet door. Sometimes he thought he heard monster noises in the closet. Sometimes he thought the door was opening. Little Barnaby was scared and began to cry.

In ran little Barnaby's mama and pop.

"Does your stomach hurt?" asked his mama.

Little Barnaby shook his head.

"What for you crying, little boy?" asked his pop.

Then little Barnaby told them about his monster shoes that ate socks and shoestrings. His mama smiled, and his pop winked.

"Sometimes," said his mama, "when shoes aren't tied, they rub your heels and make your socks scootch down inside."

"Sometimes," said his pop, "when shoes aren't tied, the shoestrings fall out and get lost." Then his pop went to the closet and got little Barnaby's monster shoes. And he got some brown shoe polish and polished those shoes, tongues and all. They almost didn't look like monsters.

Little Barnaby's mama found an extra pair of shoestrings in a drawer and she laced the shoes up lickety-split. Now they didn't look like monsters at all.

Then little Barnby's mama and pop taught little Barnaby to tie his shoes in the middle of the night in the middle of his bed.

"Make a rabbit's ear with this string," said his mama.

"Then wrap it around with this other string," said his pop, "and hunt for the other rabbit's ear and pull it through."

At last little Barnaby could do it all by himself. He fell asleep holding his shiny brown shoes in his arms.

Of course the next morning little Barnaby
tied his shoes very carefully with good strong
rabbit ears before he ran outdoors to play.

Big Roy and Baggie Maggie and Scooter
were playing Shadow Man.

"Can I play?" called little Barnaby.

Big Roy and Baggie Maggie and Scooter
looked at little Barnaby's feet.

"Bet someone tied your shoes for you," said Big Roy.

"Bet those shoestrings get loose and your shoes eat your socks again," Baggie Maggie said.

"Bet those monster shoes eat your shoestrings," said Scooter.

"Nope," said little Barnaby. "See?" And he
sat down on the bottom step and untied his
shoes and tied them up again.

"Can I play?"

"Yep," said Big Roy, running down the sidewalk. "I'm the Shadow Man. You all got to try to step on my shadow."

Little Barnaby's brown shoes twinkled in the sunlight as he chased Big Roy. He knew he couldn't catch Big Roy, so he just ran as fast as he could and thought about how good his socks felt, how good his shoes felt, what fine rabbit ears he could tie all by himself.

Suddenly little Barnaby saw his shiny brown shoes step on a shadow. It was Big Roy's shadow! Little Barnaby had caught the Shadow Man!

"Golly!" said Big Roy, skidding to a stop. "I didn't think you could run *that* fast."

"It's those tied-up shoes," Baggie Maggie said. "They help him run."

"And look how tall he's grown. Just look,"

said Scooter, standing next to Little Barnaby.

"We can't call him little anymore," said Big Roy.

"We'll just call him Barnaby," said Baggie Maggie.

"Run, run, run, BARNABY," shouted Scooter. "It's your turn to be the Shadow Man."